STAR PAWS
ANIMAL DRESS-UP

KNIGHTS
STICKER BOOK

Thou must dress me up!

Me too!

Code of Honour

I, Sir . . . .

do to hereby solemnly promise to

abide by the following rules:

- To not pick my nose in public

- To not scratch, lick, or bite myself

- To not steal or sniff what is not mine

- To eat with my mouth closed

- To cover my nose when I sneeze

- To clean my teeth before bed

- To rescue all fair maidens in distress

Signed . . . .

Perceval Page

Olivier

MACMILLAN CHILDREN'S BOOKS

Phew!

No animals were harmed during the creation of this book

What a Good Knight

As Medieval knights, Sir Flopsy of Nibbleswick and
Sir Arthur Sixpence are bold, brave, chivalrous
and always ready to fight. Except for this morning . . .

Sir Flopsy of Nibbleswick

Use your stickers and help these naked knights get dressed. Quickly, before they embarrass themselves any more!

Sir Arthur Sixpence

Shield Show!

These knights all need a coat of arms on their shield, so get decorating!

Sir Gladys Dubois

Methinks I should have ordered a smaller one . . .

Use your stickers to create some bold new designs.

Sir Mike Robe

Sir Squeakalot

Fashion Crimes and Punishment

Peter Peasant is in the stocks for having BAD dress sense.

Use your stickers to pelt him with rotten fruit and vegetables.

How very mediEVIL!

Peter Peasant

Knight School

Meet the young knights in training as they try their hand at jousting, archery and swordplay.

The Peasants are Revolting!

They really are – look at them! They've got the plague, they're covered in pox, AND they stink!

Star Paws Stickers Start Here!

For Perceval Page!

For Olivier

What a Good Knight

A complete outfit for Sir Flopsy!

What a Good Knight

Try all these on Sir Arthur!

Shield Show!

Shield Show!

Fashion Crimes and Punishment

Cover poor Peter's head!

Knight School

Outfit for Squire Mungo

Knight School

Try all these on Sir Cowardly Custardé

For Tim the Chivalrous

For jousting!

Also for Tim the Chivalrous

For Sir Nibbles

For Sir Clumsy of Clutz

Weapons!

Clumsy's shoes

The Peaseants are Revolting!

Germs & fleas

Pustules (obviously)

(Poo)

Stink

Boils!

l'eau de Ditch

A peasant bonnet!

Posh or Peasant?

Very Peasant!

Very Posh!

Under Siege!

For Sir Christopher Catflap

For Charlie Chainmail

For Terrifying Trevor

For Sir Tiddles

Under Siege!
Hats for John, Paul, George and Bingo.

← For Friar Cluck →

For Ivan Hoe →

To protect Little John!

Peasant outfit for Lance

Knights of the Hound Table

For Sir Lionel of Ritchie

For Sir Galahad Barker

For Sir Prancelot

Knights of the Hound Table

Hat and trousers for Squire Squeak

For King R. Furr

Hat for Serf Service

Hair and moustache for Sir Mordrat

Hair for Sir Fetchstick

Moustache!

HOUNDS TOOTH PICKS

Eyes open!

Knight Watch

Moustaches and beards!

Use your stickers to add bulbous blisters, warts and fleas to these smelly peasants. Don't forget their dodgy medieval hairstyles.

Ditch Dwelling Duncan

Parp Larkin

Sam and Ella

Posh or Peasant?

Who will be a courtly knight or a lowly peasant?
You decide!

Arnie

Use your stickers and decide whether it's rags or riches for these two animals.

Danny

Under Siege!

Join Sir Steven Seagull and his band of knights as they attempt to defend the King's castle . . .

These poor fellows aren't ready! Use your stickers to give them armour and weapons. Quick, before it's too late!

Knights of the Hound Table

King R. Furr and his knights enjoy a hearty feast to celebrate their success in battle. . .

Sir Prancelot

Sir Galahad Barker

Sir Lionel of Ritchie

Squire Squeak

Using your stickers, set the table for a sumptuous feast!

Serf Service

King R. Furr

Sir Fetchstick

Sir Mordrat

Knight Watch

Good Lord! These men need waking up immediately! They're supposed to be on lookout duty . . .

Blinky

Millicent

Thelma

Louise

Geoff

Use your wide-eyed stickers to wake them all up, before they get into trouble!